Sending Nudes
short stories & poetry

Edited by Julianne Ingles

Guts Publishing

"Nudity is the uniform of the other side... nudity is a shroud."

— Milan Kundera

CONTENTS

EDITOR'S NOTE

While I was editing our 2nd anthology, *Cyber Smut*, and thinking about what our next anthology might be, I was working on a short story called 'Send Nudes', a nonfiction narrative by Ellie Stewart (now Ellie Nova). The writing was experimental, a mix of prose and poetry, and as I trimmed away I found that the main underlying story was about a young woman experimenting with and trying to understand her sexuality by sending nudes. What captivated me most was the honesty with which it was written.

My favorite line is: 'I never send nudes from a happy place.'

I started to wonder: Are there millions of other Ellie Stewarts out there?

Whether a person has sent nudes or not, mainly what I wanted to know was what they think about sending nudes. But I also wanted to know why people send nudes, not that I haven't, and yes I understand the obvious, but beyond that I thought maybe it was some kind of modern-day courtship. Or something to do to spice up a boring day—lockdown comes to mind. Or maybe just a way to connect with another person if you're feeling lonely. But I also had to ask myself: has this been going on for ages, and now it's just much easier to do, and is this the age-old exploration of the beauty of the human form, like Titian's painting *Sleeping*

Venus, and is our modern day sending of nudes some diluted version of this?

If that is the case, whether a photo or a painting, is there much more to it as Milan Kundera suggests: "Nudity is the uniform of the other side... nudity is a shroud."

I didn't know if I'd actually get the answers I was looking for, but I did know this: the sending of nudes in the present day is widespread and common. And I thought, yeah, and I bet there are some ballsy writers out there who'd like to write about it.

In mid-June, I posted the call for submissions for *Sending Nudes*. By 1 October I had an inbox full of stories and poems. As I read, I discovered many different attitudes and experiences and creative takes on the topic. My questions weren't all answered but I began to understand what people thought about sending nudes, in this day and age, and what kind of meaning they assigned to this, shall we say, activity.

In the end we selected seven poems, seven short stories (five fiction, two nonfiction), one essay and one haiga (painting and poetry) which is on the cover. Interspersed throughout the anthology are quotes from the authors with their personal thoughts on sending nudes, or creating stories about sending nudes.

To my assistant, Katy Dadacz, I send an enormous heartfelt thank you for her dedication and persistence, for hours of reading and discussion, for finding stories that I had overlooked, and for helping to bring this project into its present form.

An equally enormous thank you goes to our contributors and their ballsy stories and poems. It's not easy to tackle this kind of a topic, much less publish it. So, hats off to our contributors, for their boldness, for their talent and originality, for their professionalism, for putting up with my steady stream of emails, in particular when I was gathering quotes. Which I greatly appreciate and believe has added something very special to this anthology.

If you'd like to find out more about our contributors, we've interviewed everyone – some written and some video – and posted these on our blog: www.gutspublishing.com/blog

Many thanks for your support and I hope you enjoy reading these stories and poems as much as I have.

Julianne Ingles
11 December 2020

Sending Nudes

(Here we go, ready?)

(And so we'll start with Karla Linn Merrifield, whose haiga adorns the cover of this book —'Tangibility'. Haiga being a Japanese form of art, painting and poetry, which in this case is a painting by the American artist John Sloan, from 1913, with a poem written by Karla. Today, after I interviewed Karla, I asked if she would like to write something about how sending nudes has evolved or changed over the years. The essay that follows is what she sent.)

KARLA LINN MERRIFIELD
Sending Nudes: Then, Now, Ever

Love, lust, pleasure, desire, beauty, anatomical study, self-expression, egotism... The impulse behind sending nudes are many. Creating nudes and sharing them seems to be part of human nature. Even the Ancient Puebloans of the American southwest, widely known for their pictographs and petroglyphs, have "sent" us nudes from their cliff dwellings and canyon walls, including, to my surprise, an image painted in ochre on sandstone of a couple copulating!

I imagine most readers of *Sending Nudes* grew up in a world where Western Art, from its inception, examined the naked human form in painting and sculpture, from the Greeks and Romans to the Renaissance all the way through to the modern era. I remember seeing Michelangelo's statue of *David* for the first time when I was a college student traipsing around Europe one summer. As I grew closer to the massive sculpture, tears welled and spilled down my cheeks at the sublimity of the master's depiction of the muscular male physicality of the Biblical king and poet.

Thousands of artists have sent us their nudes over the centuries, celebrating the human form in a multitude of styles that encompass Marcel Duchamp's oil painting *Nude Descending a Staircase*; Robert Mapplethorpe's sensuous photographs of male nudes; Henry Moore's hefty, smooth-bodied sculptures; and John Sloan's tender nudes in ink, pastels, oils, etchings, and pencil creations that so captivated me through the 108 haiga I created with his work, of which 'Tangibility' is perhaps my favorite.

And, keep in mind, for decades Hugh Hefner has sent us nudes every month in *Playboy Magazine*, a staple of sent-nudity that continues to this day.

Then, perhaps unique to me, there were those drawings of stooped, hairy Australopithecus "sent" to me in my high school physical anthropology textbook that stimulated my teenage libido!

Now, in the digital age, anyone can be an artist of the nude (and many of us have), and send our creations off with the touch of a keystroke. "Dick pics" and "pussy shots" are commonplace, and sending nudes has become egalitarian—sexting is widespread among both men and women. It's a cultural phenom with pros and cons. I like to believe most nude selfies are innocent courtship gestures between potential and current lovers. Alas, privacy isn't guaranteed in cyberspace. Think of the politicians and journalists who have fallen from grace when caught in the sexting act. Worse, much worse, are the young women who have been victimized by sexual predators. Still we persist.

We're fascinated by the human form because we're, well, human, and this landmark anthology celebrates that impetus. There's nothing new about sending nudes.

(What I love most about being an editor is the writers I get to know. Like Karla. She sent the sweetest email a few days ago with a recording of her 'Big Ben Tonal Poem', in which she played the guitar and sang the poem for all her British friends. It was very touching. And so, now I would like to introduce you to another poet, Michał Piotrowski, who I met in December 2019 at the Poetry Café in Covent Garden, when we had a reading for our *Stories About Penises* anthology, and the first thing he did when I met him was teach me how to say his name — *Mee-how* — that is phonetically how you say it in Polish, which I found very endearing about Michał, that he loves his name and his native language that much. After the readings I found out he was a poet, and later he sent me one of his poems. But it was not anything ordinary, just as he is not anything or anyone ordinary, but an experiment of poetry and imagery. I loved it and wished he had sent it to me for the *Stories About Penises* anthology. Eight months later when I announced the call for submissions for *Sending Nudes*, Michał sent the poem again, and my heart leapt with joy at this nude sent to me, and now sent to you, which you will see when you turn the page.)

11

MICHAŁ KAMIL PIOTROWSKI
Dick Pic

i

i

i

i

i

l

l

i

l

l

!

ASS

ASSTIC

WHOLY

HOLE

ACTION

FRICTION

FRICTION

FICTION

FRACTION

REACTION

FRICTION

SUCTION

FRICTION

FRICTION

PRICKTION

SNAP	SLAP
!!!FLIP!!!	!!!FLOP!!!
BON BON RAPT	TRAP BON BON
BOOMBOOM	BOOMBOOM
!!!NON!!!	!!!STOP!!!
TIP	TOP

(while I was putting this anthology together I kept thinking about Ellie Stewart's story 'Send Nudes', because it really was the inspiration for this anthology, and some pretty ballsy writing too. And then I decided to get in touch with Ellie (now Ellie Nova) and see if she wanted to publish this in *Sending Nudes*. To my delight, she said yes.)

"When I sent nudes to men in my early adulthood, there was a mismatch between the experience of the sender and the receiver. For the men, I think, it was a brief thrill. But for me it was an attempt to find connection and reassurance that, despite my darkest beliefs, I was lovable after all."

— Ellie Nova

ELLIE NOVA
Send Nudes

He wants more.

> Please. A naked one.

They always want more.

> You're so hot.

A copy/paste job. The same words, sent to whichever woman.

> I want to see your hot body.

When the image appears, he lets himself believe he's the only man who's seen it.

> You make me so hard.

* * *

I met Sam when I was 18 years old. I had been at university in Leeds for a few weeks and was invited to a second-year students' house party. I arrived already drunk[1]. Sam was two years older than me; his voice was low and he

---

[1] Alcohol consumed: A bottle of white wine with my flatmate Kathy in her bedroom, shots of vodka and swigs of beer with the boys in the living room. Outfit changes: two. I fell on the balcony and got my first outfit (tight jeans and sparkly top) soaked in muddy water and cigarette butts so had to put on something different (black top and boho skirt).

was tall. But he was also a little overweight and dressed so scruffy: shorts, a hoodie and flip flops, and in October. Later I found out he had gone to Eton, and had money, but he didn't dress like it.

He followed me round the house all night, through all my changing moods. I'd be chatting merrily one moment and arguing furiously the next. I found myself in a dark bedroom with a group of boys passing round cocaine, and I got upset. He followed me downstairs to make sure I was OK.

'I never do that stuff,' he said as we stood on the landing. 'Sorry that happened.'

* * *

He was the first person to post on my Facebook wall: How are you? Hope you've had a good day.

He didn't have my number yet. When his friend Martin was round our flat, eating Sunday lunch, he said:

'Sam asked me for your number.'

I sighed.

'*Fine,*' and gave it to him.

I was flattered that he hadn't given up, even though I'd made it clear I hadn't fancied him.

That changed.

* * *

Over that year we spoke often through digital means: on Facebook, MSN messenger, text. We met IRL only occasionally. But by the time the academic year was drawing to a close I was tied-to-the-mast crazy about him and he was intermittently interested in me.

In the spring, he invited me to his birthday pub crawl.

I turned up at the third pub on the route. He was sitting at a table surrounded by his mates and he ignored me. As if I was just some blonde he didn't know.

I stood in the crowded pub. He and his friends were all in matching red t-shirts with their nicknames on the back. They'd talked about it, laughed about it, when I'd been round Sam's place - but he had never asked if I wanted to wear one too. He didn't have any nicknames for me anyway.

His friends at another table saw me standing there and waved. They invited me over to sit with them.

Outside the pub, one of his friends stared at me. Open-mouthed staring. I felt exposed.

I said: 'Why are you staring at me?'

He shook himself a bit, as if coming out of a trance.

'Sorry, you're just very beautiful.'

Sam heard this.

He walked over and put his heavy arm around my shoulders. The friend was embarrassed.

'Sorry!' he said. 'I didn't know you guys were a couple.'

The drunker Sam got, the more affectionate he became. Outside The Dry Dock, a boat-turned-pub moored beside bellowing A-roads, he pulled me close to him and kissed me.

19

Someone shouted: 'Get a room!'

After that his arm didn't leave my shoulders.

We ended up in Club Mission. As lights flashed through the mist, he picked me up. My feet left the ground. Everyone could see. I couldn't believe it was happening: he'd picked me up and he was holding me, like I belonged to him.

We got a taxi back to his house and climbed up into his bunk bed. It creaked and wobbled with the weight of us both. He briefly groped around between my legs and I gave him a blow job. Then he fell asleep.

I lay in the dark with a sense of relief. Relief that he'd chosen to spend the night with me, that he hadn't left me to walk home on my own. I knew, in the morning, it would be back to grunted monosyllables, teasing comments that went over the line. But that night he was snoring beside me and I was with him and he was with no one else but me.

* * *

In the summer, I went home and he didn't call. He didn't text. He didn't message me on Facebook or MSN messenger. I begged and I pleaded:

Please Sam I miss you so much – please reply.

Sam I'm so worried you'll leave for Argentina and we won't be able to see each other. I can come to London, wherever you'd like, wherever is easiest for you.

Sam I'm sorry to be so needy but I'm just so worried that I haven't heard from you.

Have you forgotten about me? Please just send me a message, just so I know you're OK. A text, an email, anything. Please.

A few weeks later another boy, Jack, asked me out. I thought about Sam. I felt guilty. But I said yes.

One night as I lay in my single bed in my childhood room, my phone started ringing.

Sam calling

'Hello stranger,' he said.

His voice was deep, monotone - gorgeous.

'Why haven't you been in touch?' I said, careful not to sound angry or upset. 'I thought you'd forgotten about me.'

'Sorry, I've been in Corfu and the countryside. No signal.'

That didn't sound believable.

A few days later I told him, via text, about Jack. He replied:

You're a psycho.

He left for his year in Argentina two weeks later.

Still, that wasn't the end.

* * *

He tells me he is masturbating and I tell him that I, too, am masturbating but I am not. I am sitting at my desk in the room on the second floor, the house on the corner of a dark street in Leeds, blinking at a screen.

I've sent him nudes.

He types: oh my god you're so sexy fucking hell

He types: I've never seen so much cum[2]

* * *

Before sending nudes, one must prepare.
The body is edited. The body is made better.
The hair on the head bleached; the hair on the
underarms, legs and vulva removed; the face painted. The
image cropped, smoothed, filtered, rendered black and
white sometimes – when the pink shades seem too coarse.
Even for a man with his hand round his cock.
I try to be artistic. I try to make it beautiful,
the exchange.

I lay my body out on the screen.
Please take.
Consume.
Erase.

IRL: I lay my body out too. I am a sexy, compliant,
up-for-anything
plaything.[3]
I am having So Much Fun.

---

[2] Here I want to reassure you that all I wanted was love. I don't want you to think
I'm a bad person. I don't want to offend you, by writing the word 'fucking', by
writing the word 'cum'. So please: think of love, when you think of me.
[3] Always drunk at night and the next morning - I just let whatever happens,
happen.

I giggle, I gasp. I arch
my back, I toss
my hair, bend myself
over, bend myself
backwards,
stretch, open,
accept,
endure, I rarely
come.
They seem to have no interest.

* * *

A girl starts to appear in Sam's Facebook photos. A dinky little Argentinian girl with long dark hair and olive skin. She looks nothing like me.

You have a girlfriend now? I type.
Yep.
Have you had sex?
No. She's Catholic so we can't. Just dry humping.

I meet up with his friends in Leeds. We go to the cinema; we go for drinks. Rob, one of Sam's best friends, fancies me. We go to a comedy night and afterwards I have sex with him[4].

---

[4] Alcohol consumed: a bottle of red wine before leaving the house, three pints of cider, a Jägerbomb, and whatever I am given when we go back to theirs at the end of the night.

I do not fancy him at all. He is bald[5], and jealous, and says things like: 'Women don't poo, do they?' like it's a cute thing to say.

I fancy Tim, who lives in a house with Rob and his twin sister Katie. Tim does not have a lot of personality but he has a ripped body[6]. I go into his bedroom and he shows me how much he can lift.

Rob says to Katie: 'I think Ellie fancies Tim.'
I have sex with Tim.

Rob finds out, and goes nuts.
Sam finds out about Rob, and Tim – because I tell him – and everyone goes nuts.
I shut down my laptop.
I switch off my phone.
I lie down on my bed.

I realise I've lost a lot of friends.
I take a pair of scissors and slice up the insides of my thighs.

* * *

I never send nudes from a happy place.

---

[5] I am sorry for this comment. Bald men are wonderful, gorgeous humans and I am a shallow piece of shit.

[6] I told you I was shallow.

I beg many of them, later, to delete the photos. They promise me they do, but who knows?

You could find me, I'm sure, age twenty reclining in lacy underwear a little plumper than I am now, my face rounded, boozy
eyes glazed.
I hope they don't come back, I hope they aren't found, I hope I'm not
shamed.

Maybe they still use them – as an aid – maybe they conjure real
memories
in the way the women online don't, the women
who moan 'oh yeah, *oh yeah!*'
Maybe they remember my sounds
when they see
the black and white photo of my rounds and mounds but
my sounds weren't real either.

* * *

Sometimes I get things mixed up, in the same few drunk hours on Messenger – swimming from drenching pain to a window –
a possibility,
for love.

Mark types:

You're obviously not that serious about killing yourself because you haven't done it yet.

Months before, I'd said: 'Men just don't seem to have the same capacity for empathy as women do.'

Dom, who studied Philosophy with me, said: 'You should meet Mark, then. He's the most empathetic person I know.'

So I met Mark at a student union social event. He was tall and funny with soft curly hair. He was a little camp, a little theatrical – which was endearing. I looked for the empathy but after four glasses of red wine it didn't matter. That night in bed he slapped my vulva with the palm of his hand.

The next morning, as he was about to leave, he pulled back the duvet to look at me. I covered my eyes with the back of my hand.

'God, you're so beautiful,' he said.

So.

This night, online[7], I try to steer the conversation some place different. I type:

I think about what we got up to sometimes…

Yeah?

Do you remember?

Of course I do.

I want him to say I'm gorgeous. That isn't happening.

So:

Do you want to see a pic?

---

[7] Alcohol consumed: half a bottle of Bacardi Carta Blanca rum with Diet Coke.

I don't know. It feels weird going from suicide to naked pictures…

It's OK. I feel better now.

Well… I would like to see a pic.

I always like it when they're not pushy, but polite.

* * *

This whole piece, really, is a nude. Pixels dropping
into place, coming together, forming
an image of me
on my knees
leaning forward
my arms close
to my body pushing
my breasts together
my thighs slightly
apart
my mouth a little open
eyes
somewhere else.
screen
glowing.

"Sending nudes is a new form of intimacy that can feel liberating, but it also makes a gift of our vulnerability. The act says, *I trust you with this. I trust you.*"

— Claire Askew

CLAIRE ASKEW

8 ways to lie in a hotel bed alone

i.

It's a frigid March. From the striplit Inverness station
concourse I watch the last train—Dingwall, no stops—
zoetrope the curve then punch out into the night. Afterburn of
tail lights. Ice greasing the wires. They're pulling the ticket
office shutters and allocating me this bed, these walls, hospital
corners and a fire door. Lamé curtains on clicking tracks like
that late-night fishtank train: now pulling into Dingwall where
a white-gloved guard unlocks the doors for no one.

ii.

Like matches go with paraffin,
like an adjective goes with a plain, chaste noun,
like a black coffee justifies a half-cigarette,
the naked selfie was surely invented
to go with hotel bathroom light, right?

iii.

I'm taking inventory of all the things I hate:
the usual. Stomach. Thighs.
Tented grey pyjama shirt with wine
stain. Face. Six years of never having felt desired.

It's a Virgin Mary pose I strike:
the camera-phone held up to the mirror like

a Hand of Protection on a kind white
lady whose face is benevolent, whose feet
warm the clean, funereal tiles,
who is chapelled by cold,
by dull, flattering light.

iv.

You alone? I write, but I've already thumbed them from a state
of *I'll never actually* into the sent-box of *holy shit I did*, and I
think of all the places you could be right now, pulled alert by
the high ping of the *you've-got-mail*. In my head, you're in the
chip-shop queue and your mouth is wet from the salt taste of
the air, and all the fry cooks are laughing, or perhaps you're in
a bar just lifting a frosted pint in your free hand when under
the sheeny table you feel something shift, and instead of
bringing it to your lips you touch the cold glass against your
cheek, cooling the heat that's rising there, leaving a pink welt,
a crescent of damp, and imagining, for a half-second, my kiss.

v.

The bed is hard. Surely too hard
for anyone to sleep in, and the bar
downstairs has hard-
and-fast rules about football colours,
leathers, and they're painted on the hard-
board wall, and if I listen hard
enough I can hear they're calling
time and the last hard
drinkers clatter into frost already hard-
ened on the night, and it's hard
to keep track of much after that

because you write back and oh,
I suddenly feel the distance
between us: five hundred and seventy
miles of hard, hard road.

vi.

That near-dark, where the room looks like it's moving. My
eyes fine-tuning their f-stops, fingers all pins and needles, all
busy being what fingers were arguably made for. *Sext* is a
stupid portmanteau—no *sex* in this digital gloaming, this
hurried thumbprint small-screen semaphore. Somewhere
below me, a door is opened, shut—a woman's laugh falls
through the lift-shaft like a lobbed knife, waking half the
floor. I hear myself quiet the wordless hearing's-edge prayer I
hadn't known I was making, blurt a curse instead, and dial.

vii.

This whole poem was foreplay
up to now: anticipating
the stanza where the woman
listens as the man comes, her name
like sherbet in his mouth
on the static line, or like new gum,
like a song he thought he'd forgotten.
This is the plot twist, the volta
before the couplet's loosed,
the *but*, the *yet*. His breath
is wuthering the earpiece,
so she imagines him out
on a mountainside somewhere,
a stiff westerly pressing him earthward,

bending him against its element
as he climbs, and the path's
jack-knifed and lousy with scree,
and all his limbs are smiling with effort's
sweet burn, but it'll be worth it,
the view from the top of all this,
no full stop at the line end, but
more an ellipse—the enjambment
hung in the breathless white of this page
like the drop-off after the summit,
the plateau, the *oh fuck, baby, oh*...

viii.

...and the other sounds all
rush back in. Clang
of the taxi rank, the slow
night-time keen of the gulls
you can see in your mind's
eye, and the lone drunk
at the laundrette's door,
fist wringing the grille
out of time with his *will
ye go, lassie, go.*

"Concepts such as body image and reversing the gaze are important to me. All of us have been victims as well as upholders of a stereotypical idea of body and beauty. In the film *The Danish Girl*, Alicia Vikander's character (she plays a painter) says to her male model 'surrender to the gaze'. That line struck me as interesting because conventionally, men have been the ones to look at women's bodies and appreciate it or establish standards. 'Objectification' has mainly been used in the context of women. However, that discourse is now changing. I think it's also in part due to social media which has made it so easy to create and consume images."

— Shyama Laxman

SHYAMA LAXMAN
The Nudes Editor

During the day, I sit at a call centre
And say how may I help
At night, I am a Nudes Editor
I work from home, eight to eleven
I have the latest version of photoshop
And my Mac is always up to date
My rates are
£20 for minor fixes,
£35 for colour correction,
air brushing,
marks removal and
breast or butt enhancement
£50 for morphing—your face on a porn star's body

Most of my clients are women
Because they are more susceptible
To insecurity and body shaming
The other day I had a client call in to complain
That a potential date had cancelled on her
Because the topless picture she sent him
Had a few stretch marks around the waist
This woman had had a baby, you see
And she was getting back on the dating scene
After an acrimonious divorce
What a blow to her confidence
I suggested the £50 package and offered her a 10% discount

As a goodwill gesture

Every now and then, a few men reach out
Not so much to get their imperfections fixed
But as a ruse to send
Pictures of their penises
And talk dirty
Such men are immediately blocked
I am thinking of putting a disclaimer
That only gay men will be entertained
But I know that is not very inclusive
And I don't want a bad name
Considering my business is in its infancy
And the industry is set to boom

Sometimes, long-term couples get in touch
To create a special something to mark an anniversary
You would think that years of togetherness
Would surpass superficial considerations
But these clients have the longest list

I am ethical, in that, once I finish a client's job
I delete all the files
But sometimes, after a project is over
The final result is so arousing
That I can't help but touch myself
This mostly happens with the £50 package
Perks of the job, I guess
When not working, I am improving my craft
By taking my nudes
And fixing every single mark, scratch, scar

Enlarging the body parts or reducing them
Creating several permutations of the original body
I then send it to a few guinea pigs
Without my face, of course
And wait for their response

"Sex and sexualities have always fascinated people throughout history. They become fraught contested topics even more when the internet allows for anonymity, a double-edged sword. Somehow, it is important that our increased use of technology does not lead to us sacrificing our humanity and our respect, both for ourselves and for others. It is the responsibility of us all not to judge those who send nudes; those of us who receive nudes or who enjoy pornography when it is consensual. Equally, it is our responsibility to understand the dangers of pushing 'send' and to not malign others before thinking of the consequences. All of them."

— Lynda Scott Araya

LYNDA SCOTT ARAYA
The Photograph

Flaccid windbags and crinkled like old rawhide sucked
soggy by a dog,
Her breasts drooped off her chest like molten lava, both
dangerous and seductive
They lay, a noose ready for a man, or even a boy to lay his
head.
Two sharp angles pointed outwards, long compass legs that
measured desire—a ticking time-bomb.
Her mouth was a lip-stick smeared sinkhole into which men
breathed their lust,
As her toes stretched wide, pushed into the corners of the
photograph
That could have been a diagram in the Kama Sutra or a
gynaecological textbook that
Carefully labelled, pinpointed the loss of innocence and the
downfall of youth.
She and the young man poised above her with his eyes
squeezed shut
Perhaps with focus or repulsion in equal amounts
Were framed by the young photographer who looked at her
slackened belly
Slashed by the rites of motherhood and at his schoolmate's
buttocks
That thrashed and bucked above her.
They told the age-old wearied story of a schoolboy's
fantasy and of vanity unchecked.

Afterwards, she would say she had been photoshopped
That it was a trick of light but a photograph never lies and
she had worn his tie as a favour.

"Increasing social isolation and eroding individualism beyond utility makes reasonable that many strip themselves defenseless in hopes of obtaining the simplest recognition: lust, indifference, or shame. Humans are not digital code. We are animal drives, not pixels or bytes. Each aching to taste honest emotion deep, true and new again."

— Michael Wayne Hampton

MICHAEL WAYNE HAMPTON
Sex for the Quarantined

Adam's home office has no windows. His dogs yap at the door as he unzips himself. He puts a Post-it Note over his laptop webcam as he wrestles himself stiff. The dogs scratch off down the hall. He inhales deep as a free diver, strains to swell and takes the pic. He studies it, and regrets that he is circumcised. The app loads. Username and Password just launch codes now shooting one more faceless penis into cyberspace. His opens and closes his phone every five minutes. Soon the dogs will need their walk. He waits breathless for a single Like. Tomorrow he will have his prostate exam. This time it will be negative.

Ashley's husband hacks to catch his breath in the shower. She blames ragweed, and refuses to believe it could be anything else. She will force him take an allergy pill before bed. He will say she is being a hypochondriac. She misses health insurance. The water beats louder behind her bedroom wall as she buries her elbows into the mattress. Her chest dive bombs as her ass arches as high as it can before her back aches. She holds her phone in front of her face, then inches it higher, until her butt cheeks look like giant pale mouse ears behind her. Snap. She rolls onto her back, tags a peach emoji, and thumbs SEND. Thick wracking coughs steal her peace. She will give him Benadryl too. She prays the kids don't get sick when school reopens.

Frannie has a Facetime boyfriend. He lives five miles away, and thinks the virus is a hoax. Instagram posts stake him with his boys at tired college bars; none of them wear masks. Two or three times a week they video chat until he or she, usually just him, gets off detailing how hard they're going to smash once life is normal again. She loves how their cyber dates give her a reason to change out of her depressing black leggings, get made up and feel like a woman. Afterwards in bed she fumbles for her vibrator and imagines beautiful men in masks ravaging her.

You have to hold it out like a flag in a parade. You have to flex and suck in your gut. Tyler's brother broke it down: composition, angle, even lighting. He said girls are afraid to ask for what they really want. He had to have balls. They only want guys ready to make a move.

Molly never asks. Dick pics just appear like Old Navy coupons. Some flop against summer tans. Some bulge inside boxer-briefs. Some poke out from blue jeans like red-faced gophers. She turns her phone off, and mutes her AP Calculus online lecture. Scroll. Delete. Scroll. Delete. Scroll. Save. Scroll. Heart. She doesn't hate them except when her mom sees her phone go off. She doesn't really like them either. They just are. Her dog stands on his hind legs to see out her bedroom window. His head watches one car pass, then another, and another. His furry chin slumps lazy against the windowsill. And it's like that she thinks. It is exactly like that.

"I have been very conflicted about how open to be about this piece of nonfiction. In the story, I write about things of which I am not proud; big mistakes that I made. I decided to leave names and other identifying information out of the story so as to protect the anonymity of the other people involved. I am happy to own up to my mistakes, but it is difficult writing about them for others to see and hear."

— Rebekah LS

REBEKAH LS
Unthinkable

I join a photography website and create a little network. We have some connections in common, that's how I meet you. Our conversation quickly and easily turns into a cultural exchange, a Londoner and an American.

16 August 2006:

Just want you to know that I think you take the most amazing pictures – keep it up cause they are enjoyable to see. Cheers.

That is the first message I receive from you.

Our messages grow longer and longer. By April 2007, we are exchanging riskier pleasantries:

By the way, you look beautiful in your newest picture… you really should think about modeling.

Modeling…? Ridiculous. But still, your compliment means more to me than most. We begin e-mailing every day, exchanging a few normal photos, just faces, places, family. An unprecedented connection.

Three years later, exposed images are finally sent:

Another one, showing what I am working on to become a mini Schwarzenegger; long way to go, but I am willing to put the work in.

The first photo isn't necessarily… appropriate? You show off your shirtless torso and I respond with some photos of my (clothed) body. One is from behind, showing off what I had been told by a boy in middle school was my 'bubble booty'.

You type back:

Stunning, stunning picture. You really have an A1 ass. Might make that picture my wallpaper and start the day the right way.

So, you are a bum man. But I enjoy this attention from you. Time to escalate. I take some bra photos, and eventually bare breasts. I include my face in all of them. I press send. After four years of speaking to you, there is an implicit trust.

You reply the same day:

WOW your pics are AMAZING… You are so beautiful and your bosoms are A1.

You escalate it further. Dick pics. I'm impressed… and we enter a new phase of our 'friendship'. We call it 'exchanging'.

Six years in, and you are a major part of my daily life. I find teases and flirts in my inbox from you:

You've been on my mind... sexually... and I've been thinking about your "sense" of humor... also that, despite your attempts to hide it, you're v v smart. I am glad that we have met. Also would be great if you came to the UK.

I can't make it to the UK, even though it has been my dream since long before I met you. So, we continue sexting, e-mailing, and Skyping. But we are in two different countries, in and out of our own relationships. We try to keep it platonic.

One year after the offer, I finally make it to the UK. You are more than just a digital presence now.

When I lay eyes on you, I am genuinely breathless. You are even more attractive in person. My boyfriend of one year is traveling with me. You and I keep things totally platonic. I never get to tell you how incredibly drawn I am to you.

I continue my relationship with my boyfriend. You and I still speak, regularly, but less often. No sexting. Just friends.

Three years later when I visit London with my best friend, we stay with you and your girlfriend at your flat. Every time I look at you, I feel the same pull. We never speak about it but one night, alone in the living room, sitting on opposite sides of the room, when I look up after telling a joke, I can see it in your eyes.

50

I panic. I have to know.

More texts.

Me: *I know this may be inappropriate, but... I have to be honest. I felt something when we were together this year... something more than just platonic friendship. I just need to know if you felt it too?*

You: *We are good friends, and we always will be.*

Ouch. Friend zone. But that's okay. Now I can commit to my relationship and never wonder what would have happened.

I get married in July 2016.

A year later... a text notification pings on my phone:

Nobody is perfect but you are special, and I believe you are perfect for me. I didn't tell you last year because it would not have been appropriate for me to say. But I have a lot of love for you.

After my marriage falls apart (it didn't take long), you confess this. We proceed to sext, discuss the things we would do if we were together, and talk every day.

On 14 April 2018, I am back in London.

You pick me up from the airport and we spend the week together. Just the two of us for the first time. Though we share a bed, nothing happens. No touching whatsoever.

We spend an incredible week together—sightseeing, dinner, watching the news together in the evenings. It is romantic but no moves are ever made. I consider making one my last night there, but I think maybe you have your reasons, so I don't.

A week later, I find out why in a text:

You: *You were the one walking around in the towel.*
Me: *Yeah, and you moved to the opposite side of the room, so you couldn't see me.*
You: *I did move to the other side of the room… because I got hard.*
Me: *What?! Why didn't you say something?*
You: *I thought you were seeing someone at home and didn't want to be disrespectful.*

Jesus Christ.

It has been twelve years since our first encounter.

We exchange sexual videos. Me, showing off my bum. You, having a wank.

A couple days later, I go on Instagram. You are tagged in a photo, kissing someone on her cheek: *From Rome with Love. #holiday #holidaymood sightseeing #couple #inlove*

Why are you sexting me if you are in a serious relationship? Why didn't you tell me? For the past twelve years, we have talked about all our relationships. Is this one any different?

A few brief texts attempt to explain this:

You: *I have a friend who's a lovely lady. She's friendly, funny, and beautiful. She had a bad relationship in her 20s. Now she is in her mid 50s, never had another relationship beyond sexual. Lives alone, she's lonely... you are too lovely to become that person.*
Me: *I'm shocked to hear this from you.*
You: *Why?*
Me: *Because we have been sexting regularly... and you know how I feel about you. Do you still have feelings for me?*
You: *Yes. That has not changed. But I am mindful of the fact that you live in the States. So... despite having feelings for each other, I am passively looking.*
Me: *Absolutely. I have no expectations whatsoever... you were tagged in a photo on Instagram last week that makes me think you're in a relationship. I'm sorry if I have interfered with it or made you feel like you couldn't tell me.*
You: *Oh no... she's just a friend. We go way back. Tagged huh?*

You quickly change the subject.

You are tagged in more photos every few weeks: *#couple #inlove*

You start to pull away.

That same year, on Christmas Eve, you initiate sexting...
we continue each day until New Year's Eve.

Me: *When I visit in April, we don't have to do anything
inappropriate. Seems like you have a lot going on.*
You: *Inappropriate? Such as...? Anal, no condom?
Graffiti? Fly tipping?*
Me: *Hahaha, all of the above. You said you're allergic to
condoms.*
You: *Not allergic, but...*
Me: *But you want to hit it raw?*
You: *Maybe... if you want. Is that an answer? Err... as long
as you don't mind.*
Me: *I'm open, with some conditions.*
You: *Get a test before? A hot shower before?*
Me: *Worse.*
You: *Get the snip?*
Me: *Radical. Honesty.*

We discuss the Instagram posts.

You: *I don't do sex friends... never have, never will. But
currently have been spending time on/off with one girl. It is
not regular.*
Me: *Instagram makes it seem awfully regular... and
serious.*
You: *She's very cool and we have been hanging out. But
she will be moving out of the country so there is no future.*

So, I haven't been sleeping around. ...Just enjoying it for what it is... I am sorry...

Me: *Do you sext other people?*
You: *No.*
Me: *Have you told your parents about me?*
You: *Of course. They were keen to meet you but I told them we were busy.*
Me: *Do any of them know about our shared attraction?*
You: *My brothers do.*

Phew. I had told my sister I was in love with you the year before.

A few months later I'm back in London spending time with you. You ask if it's okay for your girlfriend to join us for dinner. Great.

You kiss in front of me once. It doesn't feel great.

Once she leaves, I turn to you and hit you with a big surprise: *I'm moving to London in September.*

You get tongue-tied, but say: *That's brilliant.*

On my last day, I tell you that when I move here, I want something more and quickly run out of your flat.

Five months later, I move to London.

You are out of the country with your girlfriend, on a trip you said you did not want to go on but had already made the commitment. You check on me to make sure I arrive safely.

You take me to several pubs for my birthday. We have a lovely evening, and you never mention your girlfriend. I check Instagram, and all the photos are still there. A few new ones from your recent travels… with *#inlove, #couple* staring me in the face.

You pull away.

Two months later, we text:

Me: *We don't have to get together at all. I definitely get the sense that you don't really want to be friends these days. Haven't seen you in months. I am sad about that obviously but happy to respect it.*
You: *No, no… far from it. I know I have been little offline and offish. But truly nothing to do with you. I really value you and our friendship. We have been friends for over 10 years. Don't plan on throwing that away. I promise you we will meet up soon and catch up and enjoy.*
Me: *I also value our friendship, so much. But the constant last-minute canceled plans, the ghosting when we have plans, the omissions about your life… all of these things make me feel like you don't care enough to see me or be honest with me.*
You: *A few things have happened that I have not told you. I will explain all… I never meant to devalue our friendship. I*

am juggling so much apart from the things you are aware of. Anyhow, no excuse, I am genuinely sorry.

Two weeks later we meet at a small and mostly empty pub near my flat. You tell me your girlfriend has moved in with you. You tell me how much I mean to you. It goes like this:

You: *Starting now, I'd like to spend more time with you. I have been stuck in a routine but I'd like to interrupt it so we can spend time together.*
Me: *I don't understand. What's changing?*
You: *I want to see you more.*
Me: *But you're living with your girlfriend.*
You: *Yes, but... we can still hang out. Just not at my place.*

You offer to help me fix my heating in my flat.

Once we are at my place, watching TV, you kiss me for the first time. After thirteen years. Things escalate but I hesitate... an image of your girlfriend comes to mind.

Two weeks later, we text:

Me: *I had fun, but I was nervous... and I had a lot of conflicting thoughts. It was difficult for me to relax because of that.*
You: *Of course, and I totally understand. We can explore that when you get back.*
Me: *Okay... but I have to ask. Is this purely sexual for you?*
You: *No. Clearly, I am attracted to you. But more than that... I find you intelligent, witty, and engaging. You have a*

terrific smile and sense of humour. You have compelling opinions and I want to know more. ...And sorry if I do come across as if it's purely sexual, I would not want you to feel that is the case.

Me: *No need to apologize. I just need to know because it is much more than just sexual for me. But I'm a little uncertain as to how we can explore anything given your current situation.*

You: *We can discuss this further; we will have plenty to talk about. But just so you know, there are many things I want to do with you: cinema, shopping, museums, dinner, exploring... and any sexual stuff is because there has been attraction over many years and for many I did not think it would ever be a possibility, even when we slept next to each other so. Forgive me if I get a little carried away.*

The new year begins with texts:

You: *I'll be having dinner near yours shortly if you fancy a drink later.*
Me: *Yeah, that would be nice. Let me know.*

We go for a drink. We chat. We laugh. It feels like old times. We walk back to my place, and you ask to use the toilet. Soon you are pushing me up against the wall and we kiss. I stop you.

You tell me that you and your girlfriend aren't really together anymore. She is planning to move out of the country. You are no longer sexually or romantically involved. The date is set. On the fifth of February, she's going abroad to sort out accommodations.

We end up in bed again, but I stick to some boundaries.

Two weeks later, we text:

You: *If you are free, I would love to say hi.*
Me: *Yes, come over, just drying my hair.*

You ask if you should buy condoms. I say yes... because that's the only way we can have sex, since this isn't exclusive.

You: *But this is exclusive...*
Me: *What? Do you know what exclusive means?*
You: *Yes, and this is exclusive.*

Would a man that I've known for fourteen years lie to me about something this important? Just to have unprotected sex with me? My friends absolutely think so. I struggle to imagine you are that simple and selfish.

You: *This is exclusive and... I'd like to be your boyfriend.*

We have sex for the first time. The exclusivity claim makes no sense. Logically, I understand it to be a lie.

Though you are very quick (exceptionally so), the experience itself is romantic and exciting. You are a selfless lover.

A week later, I check your ex-girlfriends Instagram.

Budapest. #travel #citybreak

That isn't where you said she'd be.

I text you to ask for a phone conversation. You call. I tell you my latest flat has fallen through, and you're very supportive. Then I tell you I'm having doubts about us. I ask about your girlfriend's Instagram.

You: *No, no, she's traveling with her friend.*
Me: *I thought she was sorting out accommodations for her move.*

You don't give an explanation but say that she is moving out and we will be together.

But you pull away.

Two weeks later, you text: *Okay going to leave in 20. Remind me names.*

My closest family and friends are visiting me in London. You have agreed to spend a day with us. To my surprise, you show up. You look amazing.

We go to Camden market and sightsee. We head to a pub, and you are your charming self with my family. We share stories and you insist on buying the first round. Finally, I think, my family will understand why I've been putting up with your erratic behavior and lies.

After the pub, you tell me you're going to pop home to send a work e-mail and then meet up with us again. I don't hear from you again for two hours.

You: *Sorry, I drifted asleep… laptop on lap.*

You have no idea how hurt I am. My family doesn't buy your story.

A week later, you come to see my new flat. We watch a film and cuddle. It feels so easy and natural.

You give me a date for when she's moving out. 19 March. We end up having sex again. You last a little longer this time (more than one pump). And the experience itself is, again, incredible.

A week before she is supposed to move out, we meet at a pub. It feels natural. I grow more comfortable and ask what will change once she moves out. You promise me more time together.

As we leave the pub, you kiss me in public for the first time. I leave this encounter thinking we will finally be together.

On 20 March 2020, we text:

Me: *So are you living alone now?*

You: *Not yet, arrangements were postponed for the time being due to the Coronavirus situation. Looking to see what alternative there is.*
Me: *What is the alternative?*

No response.

On 23 March 2020, lockdown is announced in the UK. We text:

Me: *Would you consider staying at mine during lockdown?*
You: *Yes, what are you thinking?*
Me: *...I was just thinking it would be nice for us to be together. Could watch the films we were planning on watching... I don't know if what you told me has changed, but if this is still exclusive in that sense, would be a challenge to be apart for an unknown amount of time.*
You: *That would be great.*

The next day:

You: *I have been thinking about your proposal and given all that is currently taking place, I don't think now is the right time. I mean it is an amazing idea but even the simplest logistics I cannot make work. I did not sleep last night as I was wrestling with.*

What logistics? It seems to me that anyone living with an 'ex' wouldn't want to be locked in with them for the foreseeable future. I decide to be brutally honest.

Me: *I have been relegated to the role of your side chick since December. I never wanted that. I don't think I deserve it, which is why I hesitated and set boundaries after you kissed me. But after our conversations, I decided to take a leap of faith believing that your relationship really was ending and that you wouldn't have invested over 13 years into this just for it to be a sexual adventure. I took that leap of faith because I am in love with you. We make each other happy. I can't imagine not having you in my life. I could see myself starting a family with you. You're selfless, witty, interesting, patient, and intelligent – and you know that I find you incredibly sexy (more so now than ever before in fact). But. This indefinite side chick situation is extremely difficult for me. I feel used. I don't want to be your side chick.*

I leave London to be with my family.

Four days later you text:

I love spending time with you and love everything about you. I want to be with you and see how that happens longer term but I'm not sure how it happens in the short term. I am sorry you feel like a side chick, but that is simply not the case. That is not how I operate. I'm too old for that. My status is complicated but it will be changing. And can I just say? I have enjoyed every minute I have spent with you. Every moment. Even just meeting at the pub was amazing – and hanging with your family.

I struggle to justify to my sister (and myself) why you wouldn't come stay with me.

She tells me: *He's lying. They're still together.*

But I can't let it go.

A few days later, we text:

Me*: I have been thinking about our time together. Having you in my flat and finally being together felt too good to be true. I really enjoyed even just watching a film with you... it felt like something I could get used to. And it was unbelievably exciting to finally feel your body after all these years.*
You*: I really enjoyed also. All the times we have met have been amazing. It's going to take me a while to grow accustomed to how hot you are. I've been over excited if you catch my drift.*
Me*: Well I'm willing to put in the work if you are.*
You*: Ditto.*

A week later we send photos, videos, gifs. Sexting for a decade necessitates creativity.

On 15 April 2020, we text:

Me: *I'm returning to London. Upon arrival, I have to do a proper quarantine for 14 days. At the end, however... I would like to spend some time together.*

You: *That would be amazing, yes. That sounds a great plan. We can iron out the fine points.*

You text me late in the evening and tell me you are about to go to sleep, but have something you want to do. You send a photo of your self-pleasure. We exchange, and you offer to show me live. We silently FaceTime and you finish.

Two weeks later I am back in London.

I am nervous. I haven't seen you since 12 March. I spend the whole morning cleaning my flat and getting ready to see you.

You seem to be distant in the days leading up, so when you arrive I sit on the opposite side of the couch just in case.

You ask to kiss me and eventually we sleep together again. This time, it is even better. You last longer and we change positions for the first time. You say a lot of flattering things throughout, and ask if I would be open to using condoms so that you can last longer.

We discuss you staying with me. You say it is what you want, and mention getting your mail forwarded to mine. This strikes me as odd. Later I ask my sister: *Is his ex just never moving out of the flat he owns?*

You say you will move in on 6 June.

On 5 June, I text:

Me: *Morning. How's work? Have you started packing?*

You: *Morning. Work is crazy but its Friday so I won't grumble. I have a long story for you about work but perhaps best for another day. Yes, I have packed a few things but will commit to it tonight. How are you?*

This is the last I hear from you. You don't respond to texts or phone calls. You turn off your read receipts.

You fall off the map entirely.

Nine days later I go to your building and buzz your flat. You answer.

You: *Oh, did you want to speak?*

Me: *Yes.*

You: *Meet me at the park in ten minutes.*

I walk to the park. My phone pings.

You: *Sorry, I can't do this right now but I could take Wednesday off so we can meet and talk?*

Me: *You've been ignoring me for over a week so I don't know how I'm supposed to believe that. I'm here now. You've ghosted me. This conversation will take 3 minutes.*

You: *I am getting super stressed. Can we please do Wednesday? Please.*

Me: *How do you think I've been feeling since you've erased me from your life? After 14 years, and on the day you said you were moving in with me.*

You: *I know, I just need more time to have this conversation.*

Me: *I have no assurance whatsoever that you'll even speak to me on Wednesday and I don't want any more excuses from you.*

You: *Okay. Please.*

Me: *Everything you've told me is a lie.*

You: *That is not entirely accurate and I know you don't owe me anything... but I would appreciate it.*

Me: *I'll be back on Wednesday.*

On Wednesday, I text: *Meet me at the park up the street at 5:30pm.*

As I approach, you try to hug me. I turn away.

I say: *What did you want to tell me?*

I expect this conversation to be brief but quickly realize you want reconciliation. You come clean about several lies, but say you are truly not with your girlfriend anymore.

You say: *She's definitely leaving the country.*

You say you are unsure about moving in with me permanently and 'pathetically', you didn't know how to tell me. You say you were planning to write me a letter.

Me: *So you couldn't have texted me once to say you needed time?*

You: *I know. I'm sorry.*

Me: *What do you want out of this conversation?*
You: *Forgiveness. I know I hurt you in a major way. But I would love the opportunity to show you that this behavior is not who I am.*

A month later on Instagram, I see a video of you on holiday with your 'ex' girlfriend and her entire family.

I delete all of my nudes from our app so you can't see them anymore. (I hope.)

I am left with no words.

On 16 August 2020, exactly 14 years from your first message, this ends.

(oh, I know, pretty intense. Now for something sweet.)

"...maybe we need to take off more than our clothes to be truly vulnerable. But I also think deliberately exposing our body can in itself be an act of empowerment through vulnerability, or even defiance."

— Miriam Navarro Prieto

MIRIAM NAVARRO PRIETO
I Dare You

Would you dare
to undress yourself?
Would you mind
me looking straight
at your mistakes?
Would you dare
taking off
bitterness,
cool taste,
patterned jeans,
fancy shirt?
Would you dare
showing me
your calloused feet,
broken toe nail?
Would you mind
if I saw
your wounds,
the hope,
the longing
underneath?
Would you take off
your pride, peel off
your fear
like the useless
rind it really is?
I can hardly wait
for those nudes, dear.

"When I first heard about the theme for this new anthology I of course immediately jumped to my own experience with nudes and the sending of them, and a new trend that seems to be sweeping through my friend's social media of having boudoir photoshoots taken. Some use them in social media posts, some use them for online dating, but one thing that seemed to bother me was it appeared to be strictly centered around the twenties-thirties age group category.

I began to wonder, is it my generation and younger who seems more obsessed with this idea of having nude photos of ourselves taken? Has this "trend" not been around for ages but perhaps just not in the eye of the public? Where were the older boudoir shoot fans?

Then the idea of a renegade grandmother who has always strutted to the beat of her own drum... jumped into my head and the story *Ender* began to take place."

— Molly McLellan

MOLLY MCLELLAN
Ender

It's hard to tell if it's stress or the dark ethereal blue light of astronomical dawn that wakes me. I've always loved this light. The colors of a typical sunrise haven't quite begun; the sky has barely started to hint that a new day is erasing yesterday. My stomach churns. Janet shifts in her sleep next to me. Her breathing is deep, steady, a comfort I've long had the pleasure to take for granted. It won't be long till the sky turns from a pale purple to a blistering pink hued orange, like the pith that encases the fruit of a blood orange. My phone vibrates and I snatch it up quickly to stop it from waking Janet. It's merely a reminder she must have set for me, a checklist for our photoshoot. My stomach churns again.

It was three Sundays ago when my phone went off about this same time. It was a message from my beloved Noona. I'm still finding it hard to believe she can iMessage me flawlessly when she could never quite master the digital alarm clock I had bought her for her sixtieth birthday. That Sunday I expected her usual check-in of her home, where Janet and I now resided. Her hope of returning never seemed to diminish back then, no matter how the dementia and arthritis progressed. What I received was the catalyst that led to my guts rumbling now.

As nude photos go, it wasn't heinous. I had honestly received a lot worse in my thirty-two years on this planet. What I truly could not have seen coming was my reaction.

I'm sure most people might find the image of their eighty-nine-year-old grandmother in nothing but a lace thong fairly disturbing, but all I could see was time, too much time. And it saddened me. It brought out a sense of grief I hadn't even felt when my cat Carl had passed. I thought for sure the day Noona and I buried him would have spurred something in me, but nothing like what I felt when my eyes scanned over the image on my iPhone that day.

The bad lighting, the angle of the shot, it revealed every wrinkle, every fold of skin, every scar. I wanted the image gone, erased from my head. I wanted to prove it wrong, prove that not so much time had passed. That there was still a possibility to go back, to relive our lives somehow.

I never thought in a million years that a nude photo of my grandmother would lead to an elderly boudoir photoshoot in my brand-new studio.

The lace curtains in our bedroom are twisting in a warm spring breeze. Through the walls I can hear our semi neighbors starting to rise. Soon their children will be up thundering around the stairwell, fighting as they do for who is next in the bathroom. A friendly reminder that supports my beliefs about not procreating. Janet is starting to stir. The light streaming through the window lets me know I've missed the transition from my beloved dark blue light to day. I sigh and push myself out of bed. Across from me hangs my leather camera bag; a beige tattered corner of an envelope peeking out from one of the frayed pockets. I have its message ingrained in my memory.

For My Olive,

*Who captured my heart from day one, may you capture
the joy and beauty of others… always.
Love, Noona*

The cold shower does nothing to shake off my nerves.
The smell of eggs, soldiers, and sausages wafts up the stairs
and my stomach almost revolts. I normally can't get enough
of Janet's cooking, but today I know I'll be lucky if coffee
slips past my gullet.

Downstairs she's twirling in a kimono she brought
back from our trip to Japan. She jokes often with me that
she thinks it will make the perfect wedding dress when the
time comes that I'm finally willing to say I do. Today as she
dances around our cramped kitchen, waving a spatula to one
of Taylor Swift's new hit singles, I honestly think of asking
for her hand in marriage; the thought slips out as quickly as
it danced its way into my head. My stomach refuses the
thought of taking on more stress today. As I reach for the
pot of coffee, she pats my hand away and points to a pot of
tea on the table.

"Can't have you being all shaky for the shoot," she
coos as she piles two plates high with food.

"None for me."

I pour some herbal tea from the pot into my cup and try
not to fidget with my camera bag too much.

"You need to calm down, honestly I haven't seen you
this riled since our first Pride march in Oxford," Janet sighs
as she speaks.

She pushes my plate towards me, a soldier already
dripping with yellow yolk. It makes me imagine an actual
soldiers' leg oozing with puss, and my thoughts trail off to

Gerald Watts, and whether the backdrop I've selected will be suitable for a World War II vet who's about to get snapshots of himself in silk skivvies. My stomach churns again, this time Janet hears it.

"It's going to be fine," she moves across the table to sit next to me, squeezing my hand gently.

Her green eyes always startle me whenever she gets this close. The angles of her face are sharper, clearer as she peers kindly into my eyes. They're dull plain brown, so boring in comparison to the emeralds that glitter back at me. I miss running my hands through her long purple tendrils of hair, but the new shock of black cut into a pixie style suits her just as well. I pull my hand from hers and gently rest it on her shoulder.

"If we get caught—"

"We won't," she cuts me off before I can finish. "I promise. Besides, it's like we said, we are making a stand, a statement, for their sexual rights."

She takes a soldier off my plate and dunks it into one of my eggs, gobbling it up as she pours herself more tea. I watch her eat as she smiles in my direction and my stomach eases slightly. Only her smile can make me relax, even if only slightly, it's one of her many gifts.

"Besides, it's the least we can do for Noona." Janet is careful as she speaks, eyeing me closely for a reaction.

All I can manage is a smirk as I begin to take out my two favorite Nikons from my camera bag to begin inspecting them and their lenses. Janet takes this cue and mumbles something about preparing the lights as she piles both our dishes still full of food into the sink on top of the dirty pots and pans from last night. For once, I'll leave the mess and hope the bother of it all will stay with me today, distract me.

* * *

Rightfully I should be blaming Edward Williams, he's the one who started this all. About six months ago his grandson came to visit the elderly residence he lives in with my Noona. The boy was apparently out of his mind with boredom, and instead of trying to sit still through one of Edward's not so thrilling tales of a bridge design he had developed, the lad decided to introduce his grandfather to online dating and the world of dating apps, *Tinder* more specifically. Within a few days Edward had broken down the algorithms needed to set up a site and develop an app that was able to operate on both an *Android* and *IOS*. According to Noona, I shouldn't be too surprised, after all she had shown me Edward's delightful display of engineering awards. Within mere days of his finalizing the system, the more unruly Mildred Manor residents were suddenly receiving invites on their *IOS* and *Android* devices to join *Ender*, the latest elderly geared online dating app.

When I first heard about it, I was furious. How could my beloved Noona possibly safely date? When every memory of me and our life together was falling by the wayside as if someone had opened some unknown sieve in her brain. How could she remember she even had a date planned? How was this safe?

I wanted to report it immediately but Noona had begged me to at least take the night to think things over. When I returned to our semi, distraught and smelling of a few pints, Janet waited patiently for my rant to end as I waved my phone and the nude picture of my grandmother in her face.

"Have you finished?"

I remember how annoyingly calm she had seemed to me, how peevish I felt she was being in that instant.

"Fine!" I snapped back at her, slouching into my grandmother's old sofa that Janet had reupholstered a few weeks before, getting rid of the scratchy fabric I now found myself missing in my rather grizzly mood.

"I know."

"What do you mean, you know?" I barked, my voice rising louder with every word.

Janet merely raised her hand and waited for me to slump further into the now too comfortable sofa. She proceeded to explain that Noona had called her out of concern. That after speaking to her she had decided to do her own research.

"It's sad and terrifying but true," Janet finished. "These people end up in these homes but they still crave affection, attention—"

"We give her all that!" I griped back like some petulant child.

"Physical attention," Janet pressed on, "I mean the STI rates in these places—"

"Oh god."

I'd had enough. I stood and marched my way into the kitchen, yanking the door to the fridge open so violently that the wine bottles in the door clanked together, as if they were frightened by my mood. I rolled my eyes at their shivering and grabbed myself some tonic.

81

"Where's the gin?" I asked Janet as I pulled a tumbler from a cupboard above the sink.

"You're being unbelievable, are you listening to anything I've said?" She waved the papers she had printed of the research she had done in my face.

"Shouldn't you be a bit more concerned with research for your dissertation than trying to pimp out my Noona?"

"You can't be serious."

I could see her anger starting to boil and a part of me got excited, I might not be the only one who would end up acting like a fool. I shrugged my shoulders to egg her on and continued opening and closing cupboards loudly, searching for gin I assumed by now we no longer had.

"After everything she did for you, after how she stood up for you," Janet's voice was rising.

"Don't even," I barked back, "that's not even close to the same thing."

"Really? How? How is it different? Her standing up for you when you came out? Now she's asking for help, and it's difficult and maybe not something you're completely comfortable with but you're going to turn your back on her when she didn't even give you a second thought before being one hundred percent by your side?"

"You don't know what you're talking about," I could feel my anger at its peak now, "it's not the same."

Janet shrank then, something in her crumpled as she laid the papers on the table.

"You're right, I don't."

She left that night. For the first time in three years she packed her bags and refused to even share the house with me. We had had fights before, but nothing like this. I stayed up all night and eventually gave up calling her when my phone finally died. With nothing else to do I began reading through her research. A lot of it was good but hard to digest. The thought of my sweet Noona, my hard hitting, tomboy Noona—who never took any crap from anyone. Thinking of her wanting a man in her life to woo her or date her baffled me. She had never shown any inkling before. At least not beyond the grandfather I had never known. So why now?

After two more nights I'd finally had enough and decided I was going to go and knock on the door of every person Janet knew from Oxford to London, to Calgary Alberta if that's what it took. I had crossed a line when I said she didn't know what she was talking about. The minute the words flew out of my mouth I was too spun out to realize what I had just said and how it must have rung endlessly in her ears.

Born to harsh conservative Canadian parents, Janet had known nothing but life on the streets at age sixteen when she came out. It took her years to find those she calls "family" now. Friends from the street, from more loving families, people who came together and helped support her into becoming the wonderful woman she is now. At fifteen I at least had Noona; I was lucky enough to have Noona.

I found her in London at her ex's apartment. Sarah was away at an Ashram in India. Janet agreed to house sit Sarah's cat. It was the first and I hoped last time we would ever fight like that. Today I thank every minute she forgave me, and a large part of me knows she forgave me mostly because of Noona and all Noona has done for her too. Still, as I sit in our rundown Skoda hatchback, I still want to blame a large part of all of this on Edward Williams, who is going to look great against the pale blue seamless paper back drop I've selected for him. The softbox light will help bring out those granules of grey blue in his hazel eyes. The thought that he will only be wearing a bowtie makes me pull my camera bag tighter into my chest.

"Remember to breathe," Janet instructs patiently as she backs the car out of our drive.

* * *

I want it to take us days to reach my studio but I know it only takes fifteen minutes. The only reason we are even taking the car and not our bikes is because I fumbled over backdrop choices and lighting for days while Janet has had costumes ready since last Monday. I think it was my last attempt at stalling this ridiculous idea long enough for everyone to come to their senses. If we all got caught it would be goodbye Mildred Manor for most of these folks whose families could hardly afford any alternative.

I can still hear Emily's voice, shrill and high as, half asleep, I picked up an unknown call years ago. Her voice tearing at the walls of my brain like some feral cat let loose on a bag of kibble.

"She's going, soon she won't even know where she is. What does it matter? Why would you waste your savings and Janet's hard-earned money on some private place when the NHS is just as good?"

Luckily it hadn't been Emily's place to make the decision. Even though she was Noona's daughter and my sad excuse for a mother, she had long ago been removed from Noona's will. Still, with Noona's antics of: trying to escape in the first year of her arrival at the manor, her falling into a group of elderly friends who thought pranking the staff was genius, then that she was the instigator behind this shoot, and that it had been her idea to convince her granddaughter (the professional photographer) to shoot her and her fellow *Ender* friends in boudoir shots, I worried she would be out. And Janet and I could scarcely afford another private establishment.

As we move through Summertown traffic my fears are bubbling closer to the surface and mingling with the honking, the heat of our rundown car, the gasoline stench filling my nose. Tea was soon going to be coming up on the dash in front of me if I didn't start breathing like Janet said.

I tried a shaky inhale as we turned off Banbury road and onto Wentworth and towards the luxurious Summertown home of Imogen Brown. She was a professor who had taken a liking to Janet and wanting to see the best for her and our joint future, had offered up her old garden shed for my studio. At first, I had been hesitant. I had never cared for the professor types of Oxford, especially knowing Emily's ties to the school as a program administrator. But when Janet had been accepted, as a Rhode scholar no less, my feelings towards the school and its pretensions began to fade. When I first opened the doors to the washed-out wood building nestled in the back of Imogen's overgrown garden; the ivy was coming in through the windows, there was dust everywhere, and enough years of garbage dating back to her great grandfather. I knew it would be a solid year before I could possibly make the place studio ready. But the light, the beautiful bright natural day light filtered in and made the greying walls glow. It filled the whole space with warmth and melted every last concern I could come up with.

Now as we make our way past Imogen's gate and down her graveled drive that light is calling to me. The warmth of that wooden shed is calling me home.

It takes Janet and I an hour to set up the backdrop stand. She's a pro by now, easily flitting from one side of the small space to the next, hanging the changing curtains and organizing the costumes and robes on the dingy coatrack in the corner. Before I even have to ask, she's already plugged in the two softbox lights, one set to continuous with a diffuser in place. While the other is programmed with my flash. My two cameras are unpacked, one sits on the wooden stool by my tripod the other is already plugged into the *Mac* laptop on the table behind me. I'm still fidgeting with the straps of my camera bag when we hear the sound of a van creeping up the drive. Each snap and pop of the stones as they crunch and shift under the weight of the tires makes my skin crawl.

Janet decides to start with the men first. She and Imogen have set up tables just outside the shed with chairs and umbrellas for the women to wait at. Imogen has been onboard from the start, despite my concerns, but now as I hear her offer everyone hot tea, I'm thankful I listened to Janet.

Edward and Gerald are the first to enter, followed by three other men. Janet shows them into the curtained off changing area and directs them each to their costume. She assures them that if they have any difficulty dressing she will be just on the other side of the curtain. They take turns going two at a time. Gerald is the first to dive happily into his outfit with Walters help, a fellow veteran who served in Vietnam. I take a couple of shots of the backdrop to make sure the lighting is right and turn off the continuous softbox. The natural light today is exquisite.

When they emerge, the other men chortle and whistle. Walter wheels Gerald over to the edge of the backdrop and then helps him to a chair Janet has placed in the middle of the backdrop. Gerald has on his old military jacket with his medals shining brightly and the silk boxers Janet picked out for him. Walter steps back, keeping his robe tight around his frame. Gerald gives the guys a cheeky wink before beaming at me and the camera.

"On with it then love," his gravelly voice makes me smile.

I start with long shots and ask him to undo and do-up buttons as I move from left to right. When I come eyelevel to him the light casts down from the windows and bathes him in its warm glow so his jacket is softened, and the medals glint as though each one is made of gold. I click the shutter closed as quickly as possible to capture the moment, and the flash on the softbox goes, capturing the hint of brazenness I've grown to love in Gerald's smile. The flash sends Walter reeling.

How could I have been so foolish? The sound of Walter spiraling is hard to take in this enclosed space. It takes Gerald, Edward, Janet, and the two other men to finally calm him down enough he can take some breaths. I hear myself apologizing over and over again but it feels futile as they all move Walter outside and leave me alone in the shed. Twelve years of professional photoshoots, of photography school, of spending hours in nature never spooking a single animal. Ten minutes into my first professional private portrait shots and I've already triggered a Veteran's PTSD.

I can feel the shaking start in my hands. How could I be foolish enough to come into this so agitated? I knew myself better than this. I should have slept at the studio, maybe for days and done whatever it took to get in the right mind space; meditated, hiked to Blenheim and back, found a way past my anxiety, my fears around all of this. The room starts spinning and I find myself bending to the floor, crawling my way to the wall beneath the windows.

The stars before my eyes start to shift and dissipate as I hang my perspiring head between my knees. The door to the shed creaks open and I focus my eyes on the dirt smudged wooden floor beneath my sneakers. The shuffling feet are familiar and before her hand grips my shoulder, I know Noona is the one who came to find me, not Janet. Somehow, they always seem to know which one I need more.

"Flash, really? And here I thought you were a professional," Noona chides and elbows me gently in my side, right above the top of my jeans.

I think it must be an Italian thing to be comfortable with the lumpiest bits of the body. Ever since I can remember Noona and all my Italian relatives have had a strange ability to poke you in your belly in a loving way, that makes you grateful there is plump flesh there to be prodded.

"Don't worry *la mia Bellissima nipote*, he will recover, he's *molto volitiva*. He'll be back in soon."

The shivering in my hands subsides. Noona takes one of my hands carefully in hers. I can feel her callouses press gently into my skin and I wish they would scar me. Leave their mark, their feel, so I could never forget them.

"This is not what bothers you though, is it?" she asks.

I nod and the tears start to trickle down my cheeks.

"Remember, you are brave, the bravest girl I know," she pauses, "aside from Janet."

A snot filled laugh escapes my mouth and my head rises as the breath comes back to my chest.

"I may not remember every moment, but I still remember that day you asked me the hardest question you thought you would ever have to ask," she says pressing the side of her head against mine.

I wipe tears from my face with the sleeve of my shirt.

"Now I have asked you to do something that's hard for you."

"It's not hard, it's just… a little weird, strange," my voice cracks slightly.

"Oh not this," Noona waves around at the photoshoot set up. "This is hilarious, a memory that's new, that might last longer. No, I've asked you something harder."

I want her to stop talking but I know from years of experience there's no way to get her to stop.

"By doing this, I've asked you to let me go. I'm asking you to let me go live the rest of my life so you can live yours."

Growing up with a grandmother as my only parent, and as my closest friend, made me different. It was a constant source for bullying before my sexuality ever truly got targeted. It was my home, my upbringing that got caught in that trap first. And I never once envied those "normal kids" because of moments like this. Many times I heard my classmates complain that their parents didn't understand them, couldn't possibly get them. Maybe it was the age gap between us or the extra years my Noona had on other parents, but she always got to the crook of things, she always got me. As the relief filled my heart and I felt air returning in a normal pace to my lungs, I knew as always, she was right.

"You've just never wanted this before. This other life. We've never had anything but our memories," I whisper.

"You never had a Janet before," Noona smirked.

The wrinkles in her face that could never be erased, were pressed temporarily into a smile.

"Maybe," she sighed, "it's time to stop focusing on what we are losing, and look forward to what we can create."

She places my camera bag in my hands and squeezes them tightly around the leather.

"*Eri destinato a creare*, to capture the memories, to keep them safe. And there will come a time when you might have to keep them all, but for now, we have some time to make new ones, to get in *piú guai, piú avventura*."

* * *

It took us four hours in total to capture everyone's portraits. Noona was the last. As she changed behind the curtain, Janet ushered the last of the women outside where everyone gathered and began congratulating one another. Imogen cracked open a bottle of port and everyone was in celebration mode. Inside the shed, Janet clipped a single fresh yellow rose from Imogen's garden into Noona's hair. I decided to take down the backdrop frame and had her stand in front of the bare worn wooden wall beneath the windows, where I had left some of the ivy to grow through. A pink hued light now sifted through the glass and brought out a soft plumpness I hadn't seen reflected in my Noona's skin in ages.

She stood tall, elegant and fragile all at once. It took me seconds to capture the moment. As I checked the computer to make sure the images were loading and saving appropriately, Noona came to my side and squeezed my hand.

"We aren't done just yet."

We took one last photo. It sits atop the mantle, adorned in a popsicle stick frame I made Noona when I was eight. It was one of the last photos I have of just Noona and I. Noona is in her chemise, her arms wrapped protectively around me, and the yellow rose is peeking out from the tight bun I had scrunched my hair into that day. Beside it is an array of photos. Our wedding photo: Janet in a pale blue suit, her hair grown back to its long blonde tangles, my lace grey dress, and both our arms wrapped around Noona. There is another of Noona and Janet at Janet's graduation. As well as one with all three of us in a punting boat trying our best to race away from Gerald, Walter and Imogen. In each one Noona's smirk takes center stage.

It took four months for the administration of Mildred Manor to catch on to *Ender*. Just enough time for Gerald to surprise some by finding a date with a lovely man by the name of Greg, while Walter found a rather serious relationship with a lady by the name of Sophie, and the others had likewise good luck. Noona kept her conquests to herself, although I suspect Janet knows things I was spared.

Three weeks later the administration was forced to shut the app down. Noona and a few of the others were reprimanded but only Edward got thrown out. His grandson had invested well in a new app and was able to set Edward up with excellent at home care. The others went to visit him often with Janet and I. No one ever leaked who took the photos. Five years later we lost Noona completely to dementia, two months after that, her body followed her mind peacefully in her sleep.

"I am extremely aware of the issues surrounding sending nudes now. Only 80 years ago, you could only send a photograph of yourself to your lover (as many writers did), as an exploration of the sexual body. Sometimes, words just aren't enough. However now, with sexual assaulters exploiting young girls, or women of any age by soliciting a nude and sending it out to the world, sending nudes in how it is seen today cannot be quite yet normalised and cemented as ordinary practice. The change needs to come through education."

— Katy Haber

KATY HABER
Digital Flesh

IF WE ARE PROGRAMMED, WE ARE
REPROGRAMMABLE.
PLENTY TO LOOK AT BUT NOTHING TO MAKE US
FEEL REAL.

If I am the intellect, and You are the body,
Why does it look so ugly when I press send?

Fine then,
I will be numeric and discrete.

I haven't seen You in three months,
I typed the passcode wrong too many times,
And locked myself out inside my teenage bedroom
With mothers and fathers sat downstairs,
I do not know how to feel
[NUMERIC] [DISCRETE]

Unacted promises slathered up with intention
You lap it up whilst I watch reality TV
You wanking over a digital presence
You are experiencing the event, but I OWN it
You remember and rewind
I dismember the digitisation of my body

Venus Pudica,

But my nude is my hand
down my crusty pants
Fingers rubbing my clit
(where all power and data is stored)
My tits, unsymmetrical

I take selfies of myself,
Store them
in an inconspicuous folder
I REPURPOSE (REPROGRAMME)
my body,
I do not do it for you.

AM I RESISTING?

[[Sex positive feminists proclaim that women can resist the patriarchal strategies of representation by using nudes as a form of resistance. Let us redefine the gendered definition of how the female physical body is read. Let us post selfies next to quotes of bell hooks and let us send nudes next to links for ethically owned bookshops with copies of Helene Cixous and Kathy Acker]]

"A lot o folk are prood tae say that they've seen it aw, but I hink a genuinely huv. Nudes are ten a penny oan the net, but a wee bird tellt me that before it wis a hing, bush porn wis. Bush porn? Folk would hide their porny magazines in bushes.

These days, people don't huv tae awkwardly ask the aff-licence fur their nudes, and they're spoilt fur choice. That's probably why I'm fascinated by unusual fetishes and kinks. The quirkier, the better. Naked bodies are *so* last century.

But even growin up wi the net, I couldnae tell ye the difference between a kink and a fetish until recently. Guid auld *Glamour magazine* put it best: a kink's sommat ootside the realm o 'acceptable' sexual behaviour. Whereas a fetish is an attraction tae an inanimate object but this can include body parts like feet.

Just last week, I discovered that ticklin kinks are a hing. You huv tae laugh. Literally, as the may be fur these folk. BDSM's aw the rage, and if you're no a fan o a guid tickle, it's no exactly a pleasant experience.

Ah wonder how many folk are gettin tired o clamps and whips and optin fur the quirky instead. When you've gat aw the choice in the world, you can afford tae be picky.

But fur aw kinks can make me giggle, its fetishes that ah cannae get enough o. When you take human body parts oot the equation, just aboot anythin is possible.

I'm a journalist. That's why I hink I've seen it aw. A wumman who married the Eiffel Tower, a man who likes tae give his money away fur nought in return, pretendin tae be a puppy online—boom, they're aw fetishes.

In a world obsessed wi the classic nude, how dae folk develop quirky fetishes and how dae they get their kicks? That's whit I explore in *Turtleneck Andy*."

— Emma Grae, December 2020

EMMA GRAE
Turtleneck Andy

My Granny always tellt me that less is mair, and God knows the auld bugger hud a point. Everybody remembers the first nude they wur sent.

HannahMcDonald93 is typing…

New Snapchat from HannahMcDonald93.

Then boom—fanny.

I dropped my phone, smashin it tae smithereens. I hud tae close my jaw wi my haun before pickin it up aff the flair.

We'd ainlie gone tae the pictures twice.

I'd been stealin my brother's porny magazines fur years, but nought got my heart racin mair than Mammy's fifty-plus catalogues.

A full-frontal view o a flappin fanny wis too much fur me tae handle. Stuff like that doesnae end up in porny magazines fur a reason. Whit happened tae the art o the tease? I can barely tell my arse fae my elbow let alone work oot that.

I shudder at the memory and click oantae the SAGA website.

A beamer stretches across my face. Mature ladies wi grey and salt and pepper hair huvin the time o their lives are everywhere. Lassies my age wouldnae know class like that if hit them ower the back o the heid.

It's no that I've got a granny fetish, well maybe a bit, but it's fur fully-clothed ladies, and I know nae lassie my age will stand fur it. No when the chat turns hot and heavy. Snaps o chebs are just as bad as fannies. I'd ainlie want tae see them in the flesh and efter I've put a ring oan the lassie's finger.

My phone buzzes. It's Davie.

"You seen whit Suzie fae school is up tae these days, Andy? Lost hur joab because o the coronavirus and now she's oan OnlyFans. Tae hink we used tae sit beside hur in maths…"

"OnlyFans?"

"You been livin under a rock, pal? It's like Netflix fur nudes. You pay a fee tae get unlimited snatch fur a month."

"Huv you heard o PornHub?" I ask.

I'm partial tae the odd scroll through the Mature category—before the scants come aff.

I'm a man o faith, which isnae an easy hing tae be these days. It's sommat I keep tae myself an aw. My pals would take the piss oot o me if they knew whit I got up tae oan Sundays.

"You can chat tae the lassies oan OnlyFans and ask fur personal content, anythin really," Davie continues. "It's got the personal touch."

"Oh richt. But I'm no payin fur Suzie's nudes."

Davie launches aff intae a tangent aboot the footie, but I cannae stoap hinkin aboot whit he said… porn wi the personal touch.

I'd never considered payin fur porn before. I'd given up oan anywan fulfillin my *very* specific fantasy a lang time ago. But this… maybe it's the answer.

God knows nae wumman's helpin me get my kicks o hur ain accord, and I'm savin myself fur marriage fur a guid reason. Mammy hud me oot o wedlock. I'm no riskin daein that. Marriage is sacred fur a reason.

I'd naewan tae cheer me oan at sports day; naewan tae teach me how tae use a razor. My Daddy wanted nought tae dae wi me when I finally put a name tae the bastart. I wouldnae wish that oan my worse enemy, let alone my wean.

"I need a slash," I say, endin the call. "Chat soon."

I google OnlyFans. But my heart sinks efter a few clicks. Nudes, nudes, nudes and mair bloody nudes.

I'm oan the wrang side o twenty-five. Hauf these lassies look like teenagers. Naw. This just feels wrang.

Wan o them hus a link tae another website: AdultWork. It's got a bit o everythin. There's escorts, folk who dae phone sex, erotica, and webcammers...

It's worth a shot. I pick a username. TurtleneckLover90. There will be nae confusion aboot whit I'm efter wi that.

Miss Barry. That's where my turtleneck fetish began. Motherwell. 1998. The auld witch micht o given me tellin efter tellin fur no learnin the alphabet fast enough, but I couldnae concentrate. No wi hur turtlenecks distractin me fur six hoor a day. She wis like a sexy ostrich, almost auld enough tae be my Granny, and I've never been able tae get hur oot my heid.

I enter a chatroom o a lassie who calls hursel YummyMummy64. She's forty-two-year-auld and in the MILF category. It's mobbed.

Beep.

Show us your boobs.

Beep.

101

How are you, babe?

Beep.

Do you do meets?

Beep.

"Do you have a turtleneck?" I type.

I look oot the windae. It's the middle o summer. I'm chancin my arm, but everybody's got needs.

"Oh, I'm sorry, I don't," she says, smilin.

But she doesnae laugh at me, and nae wonder. I've a look at whit the others are askin fur. It's the first time I've felt normal aboot my kink.

I have a Kleenex fetish.

Beep

Can I electrocute myself for you?

Beep.

Have you got stockings?

Clichéd, I hink.

Beep.

Bareback?

That's surely no whit it sounds like, I hink. Dirty, disrespectful bastarts. I click aff YummyMummy64's chatroom.

But I persevere, makin my way through efter profile efter profile until I go doon the custom content rabbit hole and end up oan a website called PantyDeal.

The biggest online marketplace for buying and selling used panties.

I click 'buy used panties'. There's nought tae be ashamed o in likin them, but this website doesnae just cater tae the young fanny sniffers, it promises 'glamorous' ladies o all ages. Maybe… just maybe.

Come oan you bugger, I hink, registerin fur yet another account. TurtleneckLover90. Again. I click oan 'ads'. Socks, mair socks, feet photies, and some lassie is even tryin tae flog a 'custom pussy coronavirus mask'. Well, you huv tae haund it tae hur fur creativity.

My heart sinks until I see an option that reads: 'general used clothes'. I click then click again. Click. Click. Click. Oh my God, I hink. It's the Holy Grail.

Used turtleneck. £20. MaureenMILF. Age 58.

You dancer.

(22 Dec 2020: often times there are writers that I don't really know that much about, so I don't have some story to tell you here but I did interview Glen Armstrong a few days ago and we had an interesting, shall we say intellectual, conversation about sending nudes although I seem to remember I hadn't yet hit the record button which was a shame and so after we finished I asked him if he would like to write down some of his thoughts about sending nudes. Now awaiting Glen's email, and if it arrives I will put it in here. 23 Dec, no email, sorry, which isn't his fault, really it's mine, me hounding the writers saying – can you send a blurb, like now? Ridiculous me. 24 Dec, alas, it arrives.)

"I wonder if there is any human activity more inclined toward contradiction than the sent nude. That body in a rectangle is at once a beginning and an end, an offering and a request, a crime and a liberty, a kitschy novelty and restoration of the past's most sacred artifact."

— Glen Armstrong

GLEN ARMSTRONG
Today's Photography

Is yesterday's photography
people taking off

their shirts
and getting comfortable

with each other in a room
where vaulted ceilings

send the message that this
is business as usual

sister
I tire of sifting

through images and sequences
implied by the sifting

dispensed by few
some of us put our shirts

back on and some of us
strip down further.

"We do strange things if we can come up with a justification for them. So much lies in the narrative, in the self-rationalisation. When thinking of the reasons why someone might send nudes, few of them matched what I myself could imagine (both for me, and for any character I could write). But science? What could be nobler! Though, once you've broken through the barrier... what then?"

— Liam Hogan

LIAM HOGAN
The Giver

I am a giver.

I do not intend that as a *boast*. It is merely a statement of fact: giving is very much part of my emotional make up. Nor am I talking about money, though I have my favourite charities and contribute whenever I'm feeling wealthy and generous. No, I'm talking about something more personal.

I give myself. For free.

On my two jackets, one summer, one winter, I wear blood donor badges. The lighter, less frequently worn summer jacket gets my gold fifty, now a few years and a number of pints old. The longer black winter jacket sports the even older but more elegant silver design, my reward for twenty-five donations. Joining it on the lapel is my Antony Nolan badge, a far rarer pin that identifies me as a one in a million, bone marrow donor. Giving marrow via stem cells harvested from my blood, with a line out of one arm, another line into the other, a fridge-sized machine whirring away in between, almost felt like a cheat, but a welcome one. I am moderately squeamish. A needle, I tolerate. Two, even. But the rest of me, my spine included? They can have only after my death.

Because I give and because of course I carry a donor card—who doesn't?—it's always in the back of my mind that my body might be shared, and so I *don't* do certain other things. In half a century I have collected zero tattoos, not even a small one. No piercings either, though that is still fairly uncommon for the average British male. I've never taken drugs of the sort you need to inject. Nor the ones you *don't*, so maybe I'm just plain boring. That's okay; mind altering substances have never really appealed. I have no desire to be anyone other than who I am, even if, as I'll freely admit, that's not always so great. Maybe that's why the thought of someone else walking around with my stem cells keeping them alive is so reassuring. They might even be having a better life than I am. Without me, they wouldn't be. Which is nice.

In addition to blood and stem cells, I also sign up for scientific surveys and University DNA research projects. Especially now, when I have too much time on my hands. I'm currently engaged in Stage 2 of the Track Covid study, which involves sending a monthly sample of my blood in the post. Though, alas, I have no access to the results. I have pricked, or had my finger pricked, for science more times than I can recall. And still I wince, both before and after the lancet stabs me.

Four years ago or so, I had my head 3D scanned at a Science Museum Lates. Painlessly, thankfully. It was part of an academic project to build up a library of faces that could be used in reconstructive surgery. I sat as still as I could, with my chin lightly resting on a cushioned pad, as an oversized camera tracked an arc around me.

It was weird, looking at the computer-generated results as the next volunteer took their turn. You only normally see your face from a narrow range of angles, the ones presented to you by a bathroom mirror. Or you might glimpse it in profile, in a photo, say, but then it is static. I tilted and panned the 3D image back and forth, vaguely repulsed by my own appearance, my face a touch too gaunt, the nose a little too large. And then I forgot all about it.

* * *

The email came out of the blue. I'd given my consent, my contact details, but never thought they'd be used. After all, I was just one of over six thousand the project had recruited, and the same anonymity that meant I wouldn't know even if I tested positive for Covid antibodies, meant that there was no direct link between my facial scan and my name.

But there *was* a link between my name and my being the sort of person who helps out a worthy scientific endeavour.

Dear Mr Hogan, the email began. *Thank you for joining the Face Soft project at the Science Museum. Your contribution has already helped researchers in a number of fields, from reconstructive surgery, and evolutionary studies, to facial recognition software.*

I have to admit the last gave me pause. The idea that an AI might have been trained on my face, that I might have inadvertently helped the Orwellian police state that seems forever just around the corner but has probably already arrived...

We were wondering, the missive continued, *if you could help us in a new project with similar aims. If you are willing to help and have access to an iPhone X, please click on the link below.*

After checking as far as I could that the email and the link weren't some elaborate phishing scam, I shrugged and, having nothing better to do since I was still furloughed, clicked through.

It took a couple of coy paragraphs about my rights to say no, data protection, and an insistent repetition that no offence was intended, before I realised what it was they wanted to scan this time.

My genitalia.

I suppose I shouldn't have been *too* surprised. What other body parts were they likely to want to reconstruct? Hands?

I imagined some booth at the Science Museum where I would be encouraged to strip off, presumably after a few drinks for courage despite the privacy screens. But no, technology had come along in leaps and bounds, or it had if you had the latest generation of iPhones with their depth detection cameras.

This was a do-it-at-home project. Appropriate, given we were at the tail end of lockdown. All I had to do was to download an app that helped stitch the data back together, find somewhere as brightly lit as possible, and slowly pan the camera across the target area.

Or get someone else to do it, the instructions helpfully suggested, but *that* was a non-starter. I wasn't even in a bubble, let alone a relationship.

I have to say, I slept on it. Twice. Before I relaxed and downloaded the graphics software. There was definitely something taboo about the project. Subversive, even. Not only had I never sent someone a dick pic, I'd never even taken one, let alone in glorious 3D.

And, like my face, I guess I only ever really see one angle of my genitalia. I'd read somewhere that it isn't even the most flattering aspect, that looking down foreshortens things, which is probably why you should never compare sizes in public toilets.

Though that was generally the last thing on my mind as I stand at a urinal. Staring straight in front of me as I try my best to ignore anybody and everybody else was more my usual play, conjuring up thoughts of waterfalls to overcome performance anxiety.

But the idea of being able to see my penis from different angles was intriguing and, ultimately, the main reason I decided yet again to step forward for medical science, if medical science would have me.

I had to re-check the instructions, read them at a more leisurely pace. What state was my penis supposed to be in? This seemed key. Flaccid? Erect? Or somewhere in between?

Apparently, all were valid options. I had merely to state which it had been, in case the researchers couldn't tell.

I didn't feel comfortable about the erect option. It wasn't that I was embarrassed by my penis. From what limited reports I have received (volunteered, never asked for), it was nothing to be ashamed of. But an erect penis is automatically erotic, even if that isn't the intent. Or maybe intent *is* the problem?

On the other hand, there really wasn't much to it when it was completely just stepped out of a cold shower flaccid. I wasn't one of those guys who pack a lunch box whatever the hour of day. This too was nothing to be ashamed of; who cared how small it was when it wasn't erect? I certainly didn't.

Except, I supposed, when it was being seen by others, anonymously or otherwise. I didn't want anyone to get the wrong idea, the wrong end of the stick. So a semi it would have to be. The sort you could still pee through, without it being an ordeal. The sort of partial tumescence inspired by thinking what they must be requesting the *women* on the register to scan... Ah, but that was too strong a thought, and I had to take a short break. Best remain detached, if I wanted to maintain a semi. Best not let my mind wander *quite* so freely. Though that was proving tricky. In short order I'd summoned up and dismissed the following thoughts:

I'm not circumcised: did that matter? Presumably not; no mention was made of that in the instructions.

What sort of person needed reconstructive surgery on their genitals?

One hopes, one *assumes*, they don't intend to create dick recognition software. But if they did, how accurate would it be? One of the things the email mentions is that the quality isn't required to be as high as in the facial scans. There's less *structure* to a penis. Which, presumably means, less identifying features. Could Google run a reverse image search on an unwanted dick pic and identify the perpetrator? Would you have to lower your pants for a dickshot as well as having a mugshot and fingerprints taken if you were arrested?

I realised, possibly belatedly, that I'd never get anything done at this rate unless I just got it out of the way. Whole days had vanished during the lockdown with nothing more significant to show for them and already the morning had morphed into mid-afternoon without notice.

Taking a few deep breaths, moving my chair closer to the brightness of the window (garden facing, not street), I activated the app and, holding the phone steady and my legs apart, I pressed record.

* * *

It took a while for the scans to upload. I half-heartedly did other things, checking on the progress bar every so often, plugging my phone in to charge when I worried the software might be draining the battery.

And then it was done, it was over, and there's a thank-you message, and...

Nothing else.

No picture no 3D image no nothing.

This was a *serious* disappointment. And, like not knowing my Covid results, while I do these things for free, for the good of humanity, I think it is beholden upon the organisers, in some small way, such as the plastic cup of tea and a biscuit after giving blood, to show their appreciation. To share the results of my generosity, back with me, not as payment, but as a token of good will.

But the scans I'd taken were not digitally reconstructed into an accurate 3D model on my phone. Apparently more powerful software was required. Which was why my data had been transferred in raw form to some university server somewhere.

This inspired a moment of rage, with a lengthier dull funk come-down, that I admit I am not proud of. That, thankfully, there was no-one to see, or hear. I contemplated changing my mind, withdrawing my permission. But that would be childish, possibly petulant.

Then, as I stomped into my kitchen and flicked on the kettle with rather more aggression than it required, I realised I could always take *conventional* pictures. They might not be fully 3D, but I guessed that didn't really matter.

The kettle went cold again as I took an even dozen photos, from different angles, on the same brightly lit chair. I laughed when I looked at them. Other than the ones from above, it didn't really look like me at all. It was pointier, for starters. Who knew? And from the side... is that an old man's penis I had? Not helped by the greying pubes and the sagging skin of something neither one thing nor the other.

I repeated the experiment candidly, catching myself off guard, as it were, as flaccid as it gets, and then once more, after a quick scroll through the plentiful porn available with even only a mildly risqué Google search.

To look at the three sets in better detail, I loaded them to my computer, and sat there for a while, flicking through them, well deserved cup of tea in hand.

But my amusement faded with the afternoon light. How very sad it was, I thought, as the day gave up the ghost, that I had no-one to send them to.

"I used to be on Tumblr as a young teenager before they did a ban on all this and you'd be scrolling through and there would be these nudes or random clips of porn, it would just come out of the blue, and you would kind of accept it because you were seeing it so much. And because it's so commonplace now, I think people forget that it is an unusual thing. And the amount of time it takes to construct a painting or a statue, and the amount of artistic vision that goes into doing that, whereas when you're just snapping a picture of yourself that lack of time means that we have a very different result."

— Issy Flower

ISSY FLOWER
Marble

John liked to take her to art galleries to stare at naked women. It was always the first place they went—past the landscapes without a glance, no time for the impressionists, no kudos for the Cubists. Just straight to the Pre-Raphaelites, and the Pre-Raphaelites when they were painting nudes. He would drag her by the hand, an over-eager child, spreading his sweat and gunk on her as his woolly fist clenched around her open hand. Then he would stop with the cool calmness of a man in his own domain, and his eyes would drift, soft and gentle, to an erect nipple.

Sarah hated it.

Every date for six months—nudes. Nude portraits. Nude statues. They would sit in the museum café and he would lecture her on things like structuralism and brushwork, when all the time they both knew he'd just been looking at boobs. Because she watched him. She never looked at the paintings. Only at him. Tracing the lines of his mouth as they pursed into a private joke at the tuft of pubic hair on one woman—the pathways of his eyes as they moved from lips to breast to neck—the twitch of his hand which opened and closed against his corduroy trousers. He rarely said a word to her or asked her opinion. Just twitched his fingers against her hand, pulling her on to the next lewd display.

Gallery to gallery, museum to museum, stopping to take in nothing but nude women who had died long before either of them had been born. Then a flat white for him, a mocha for her, drunk over two hours, returning home on the Tube in silence. He'd go into their bedroom.

She'd make a strong black coffee, drink it, then think about taking a knife to his vinyl and smashing his busts of famous painters against the wall.

Then he broke up with her.

* * *

Here, now: the pat-pat of rain, the stink of London, herself, small and pointless, standing in front of the portrait gallery, just breathing. Taking it all in. The stone façade and the woman on the door smiling as people went in. Crowds of school kids and art students in faded bralettes and oversized shirts stuffed with baccy; lone old men with bent hands twisted behind bent backs; other young women, thin and in long coats, clutching tote bags tight to them like talismans. People who wanted to be there, people alone, people like her.

But they wandered through the doors and into the corridors like John, knowing their place and their role amongst the objects. All Sarah knew were pornographic alcoves where young men idled and stared like the painters had stared in the act of painting: pretending to be concerned with colour but really looking and looking and wanting and taking. Her feet carried her there anyway—right to the statue of the Madonna.

Huge breasts, shaped and hanging like they were real, suspended in marble. Thick thighs swooped in fabric. And for once she really looked at all these things because she was the only one there. It was a Tuesday, three weeks after, and her lunch break, and rather than sitting on a park bench with soggy, clingfilmed sandwiches she had thought 'fuck it' and went to his spots. His bar, his theatre, his gallery. She stood in all his places and thought right over him.

Her thoughts now threw themselves like sick over the statue, and she watched them reform the huge tits and huge thighs to something quieter: a female model, maybe rich maybe poor, willing or not, sitting on a chaise longue draped in grimy artist's calico, waiting. Lying there for hours, being nothing but beautiful. Something that people could place themselves onto. Their object.

Her mind reshaped it again. The fabric turned an ugly vintage brown and the hair grew close-cropped and the delicate, chubby chin became swathed in stubble. The breasts sunk back slightly into a Fall Out Boy t-shirt that was definitely ironic and the thighs shrunk until they were hardly there. John was sitting there, dead-eyed in marble, on his plinth.

They stared at each other.

Sarah took off her clothes.

They hung in the air for a second, then drifted down the corridor, not to be seen again. These silks and light cottons perfect for the stuffy office just dissipated like light and became nothing. She did not look around. There was no one there. Just her, and John, and her bra and belly-control pants, tugging her in. She blinked and they were gone.

John's eyes stayed resolutely on her face.

She walked towards him, steady. The gallery floor was cold, smooth stone, planed like ice. She walked right up to him, her toes marking the floor one by one—delicate, receptive, placed perfectly for impact. Thighs and arms worked together and swished like curtains blown by the wind. Swish, swish, stop. Dead stop.

His marble eyes on hers.

'Look at me, John. Look at me.'

His eyes stayed on her eyes.

'Look at my mouth. My neck. My tits. My legs. My pussy. Just look at them.'

No.

Her own face, tracked with tears and dust, reflected in his. Eyes still on face. Hands clasped demurely, not reaching, not clenching. Throat still. Mind still. Not racing.

123

She knew what he looked at when he got home.

She could taste coffee in the air.

She sucked it in, one big breath in the lungs, filled, filling, bursting, and she raised her hand and brought it down on his head.

Marble hitting stone, records smashing, busts demolished, piecemeal on the floor.

Her naked, breathing, still holding the gaze of his smashed eye.

Her dressed, in front of this big beautiful stone woman entombed in gazes upon gazes.

Sarah envied her.

Soft, precise steps. She went right up to the tombstone woman's face. She paused, checking briefly for security, then put her eye right up to that of the Madonna. Gazed in. Placed her hand, delicately, on her exposed breast. Felt the sweat of a wool hand soaking through the stone. Saw his eye in hers.

A hundred other weather-beaten eyes peered back.

She dropped a pound in the donation box on her way out.

"Of course, it is a great way to show your desire –
especially during these times... [but] The horror stories of
(mainly females) being sent unsolicited pictures is another
issue. I don't think there should be a call for censorship but
definitely a better education system put in place for young
males about consent."

— Edward Ginn

EDWARD GINN
Easter Island Head

In the gift shop
of the sex museum in Amsterdam,
lying under a bed of dildo pencils and condom erasers
(rubber rubbers),
a couple find a postcard
of an Easter Island Head.

The cashier makes it clear that the postcard is not meant to
be here.

Do you think it is to do with the double meaning of the
word
Head
That someone left it underneath the X-rated stationery?
Or maybe a gonad obsessed nomad dropped it mistakenly?

Anyway.
They discovered they had bodies when they dug down
deeper.

(the end)

CONTRIBUTORS

Lynda Scott Araya lives in a beautiful heritage house in rural New Zealand. She has a background in education and has taught in a diverse range of settings including at tertiary level and in men's prisons. Her passion, however, has always been writing. Recently, she has been published in *Chaos*, the *Blue Nib*, *Mindfood* and *Prospectus A Literary Offering*. She has work forthcoming in *Landfall* 240.

Glen Armstrong holds an MFA in English from the University of Massachusetts, Amherst and teaches writing at Oakland University in Rochester, Michigan. He edits a poetry journal called *Cruel Garters* and has three current books of poems: *Invisible Histories*, *The New Vaudeville,* and *Midsummer*. His work has appeared in *Poetry Northwest*, *Conduit,* and *Cream City Review.*

Claire Askew is the author of *This changes things*, published by Bloodaxe in 2016. The collection was shortlisted for an Edwin Morgan Poetry Award and for the 2017 Saltire First Book Award, among others. Claire is also the author of three novels, all published by Hodder & Stoughton. Her debut, *All The Hidden Truths* (2018, Hodder) won the 2019 Bloody Scotland Crime Debut Award, and she has been twice shortlisted for a CWA Gold Dagger Award. She was the 2017 Jessie Kesson Fellow and Writer in Residence at the University of Edinburgh from 2017-2019.

131

Issy Flower is a writer and actor, going into her third year at Durham University. Her journalism and prose writing have been published by *Palatinate*, the *Bubble*, *From the Lighthouse*, and *Lucent Dreaming*. Her writing has been performed by JustOut Theatre, Kickitdown Productions, RapidReel, Sedos and Castle Theatre Company, and won 'Best Writing' at Durham Drama Festival 2020. Upcoming publications include features in *Stonecrop Magazine* and the *Common Breath 'The Middle of a Sentence' anthology*, as well as a commission as part of the BBC New Creatives scheme. She enjoys wallowing in nostalgia and keeps up a healthy twitter feed at @IssyFlower.

Edward Ginn is originally from Merseyside and moved to South East London to study Comparative Literature at Goldsmiths. When he is not writing poems or stories he is a stand-up comedian and comedy writer. He also works in a high school supporting SEN students.

Emma Grae is a Scottish author and journalist from Glasgow. She has published fiction and poetry in the UK and Ireland since 2014 in journals including *The Honest Ulsterman*, *From Glasgow to Saturn* and *The Open Mouse*. Most recently, her work was selected to be performed by Liars' League at two of their London-based events in 2020. Her first novel, *Be guid tae yer Mammy*, is being published by Unbound in May 2021.

Katy Haber – Kat/y/Haber – is a poet, writer and artist residing in London. Their real identity is manifested in the digital sphere. Their body is currently a full time student and activist, working in gender and queer culture studies. They hate TERFS, fascists and racists. For now, they philosophise, eat and sleep when not writing as a self-created AI.

Michael Wayne Hampton is the author of five books. His criticism, essays, fiction and poetry have appeared in *The Southeast Review*, *McSweeney's*, and *Rust+Moth* among many others. He can be reached via his website michaelwaynehampton.com or Twitter @motelheartache.

Liam Hogan is an award-winning short story writer, with stories in *Best of British Science Fiction 2016 & 2019*, and *Best of British Fantasy 2018* (NewCon Press). He's been published by *Analog*, *Daily Science Fiction*, and *Flame Tree Press*, among others. He helps host Liars' League London, volunteers at the creative writing charity Ministry of Stories, and lives and avoids work in London. More details at http://happyendingnotguaranteed.blogspot.co.uk

Shyama Laxman has an MA in Creative Writing from City University, London. Her areas of interest include gender, sexuality and LGBTQ. Her work has been published in *The Quint*, *Huffington Post*, *Muse India*, *Gaysi* and *ShethePeople TV*. She has written a rubbish draft of her first novel and wonders if she is even cut out to write fiction. She lives in London with her husband, two cats and 31 house plants. She loves the cats and tolerates the plants. If ever she is on death row, then she'd want Rice and Dal as her last meal. And the one thing in her handbag that she 'cannot live without' is a lip balm, like those famous women out there.

Rebekah LS is an American teacher in London with big dreams of owning a big dog. Rebekah writes about the only thing she really knows: her life.

Karla Linn Merrifield is a nine-time Pushcart-Prize nominee and National Park Artist-in-Residence with 800+ poems appearing in dozens of journals and anthologies. She has 14 books to her credit. Following her 2018 *Psyche's Scroll* (Poetry Box Select) is the 2020 full-length book *Athabaskan Fractal: Poems of the Far North* from Cirque Press. She is currently at work on a poetry collection, *My Body the Guitar*, inspired by famous guitarists and their guitars; the book is slated to be published in December 2021 by Before Your Quiet Eyes Publications Holograph Series (Rochester, NY). She is a frequent contributor to *The Songs of Eretz Poetry Review*, and assistant editor and poetry book reviewer emerita for *The Centrifugal Eye*.

Molly McLellan is a research nut to say the least. It never seems to fail that her pieces of fiction always end up leading her down the endless rabbit hole of sources, upon sources, upon sources. Perhaps this is why she felt the need to obtain a master's degree from Oxford in Creative Writing. Combining her two great loves of research and writing fiction in a place with one of the world's largest libraries and oldest collection of books. Now back home in Canada she spends her days writing, out adventuring with her beloved dog Jack, and generally avoiding the mythical land known as "adulthood".

Miriam Navarro Prieto (she/her) is a Spanish artist who drifted from performance art to drawing, currently mainly focused on writing poems and short stories on autobiography, ecology, gender and queerness. Her first self-published poetry chapbook is titled *Todo está vivo*, also available in English as *Everything Is Alive*. Her poetry in English has been featured in journals like *Ayaskala* and *Capsule Stories*. She sends out a bilingual newsletter twice a month on her creative process, plants and translated poetry: https://tinyletter.com/miriam-navarro-prieto

Ellie Nova recently completed an MA in Creative and Life Writing at Goldsmiths University. She previously worked in fundraising and communications in the charity sector. Her non-fiction, poetry and short stories have been published in various places online and in print including *Goldfish Anthology*, *Her Stry* and *Popshot Quarterly* — you can find out more at www.alittlefantastic.com. She lives in London and is working on writing her memoir.

Michał Kamil Piotrowski is a poet living and working in London. He writes mostly experimental, visual and technology-powered poetry. He enjoys making poetry interactive and he mostly works with found text. His interactive book *The Cursory Remix* has been co-written by Google Translate and is available to read on issuu.com with a print version forthcoming from Contraband Books.

COPYRIGHTS FOR INDIVIDUAL TITLES

ABOUT GUTS PUBLISHING

Established in May 2019, we are an independent publisher in London. The name came from the obvious—it takes guts to publish just about anything. We are the home to the freaks and misfits of the literary world.

We like uncomfortable topics. Our tagline: Ballsy books about life. Our thinking: the book market has enough ball-less books and we're happy to shake things up a bit.

Sending Nudes is our third anthology. It is preceded by *Cyber Smut* (Sept 2020), a collection of fiction, nonfiction and poetry about the impact of technology on our lives, our sexuality and how we love. Our debut anthology, *Stories About Penises* (Nov 2019), is a thoughtful and literary collection of fiction, nonfiction and poetry about, well, exactly what it sounds like. To quote a prominent Australian author, 'Quite possibly the best title of the year.' We think so too.

Our debut memoir, *Euphoric Recall* (Oct 2020), is a raw story about a Scottish working-class lad and his recovery from addiction and trauma. Full of grit and hope. Well done Aidan Martin.

Our website: gutspublishing.com.
Our email: gutspublishing@gmail.com

Thank you for reading, and thank you for your support!

CPSIA information can be obtained
at www.ICGtesting.com
Printed in the USA
LVHW090807150321
681564LV00008B/409

9 781999 882389